Reading Together

Advance Praise for Katarzyna Bartoszyńska's *Reading Together*

What kind of knowledge do you make in a book club? Or, for that matter, in a classroom? A barfight? A dinner conversation? Postcoital whispers? An online post? *Reading Together* is a book that tugs at the strange dialectical knot that binds the more authorized spaces of reading (the seminar, the lecture) to the differently sociable scenes where books, with all their tumult and beauty, enter our lives. With an enthusiast's agility and a patient discerning love, Katarzyna Bartoszyńska reminds us how reading, too, is a way of living in the world.

—Peter Coviello,
author of *Is There God After Prince? Dispatches from an Age of Last Things*, and *Long Players: A Love Story in Eighteen Songs*

A tribute to the company that we keep—in book clubs, college courses, incarceration, and anywhere where readers collect—*Reading Together* delves into the messy and necessary constructions that we make when we enter into conversation with a work of fiction. At the heart of this assay, which follows Kasia Bartoszyńska's professional and literary development, is a brilliant meditation on how difficult it can be, truly, to "get out of [your] own way" in a communal experience like a book club, for reasons that are learned through institutions or self-imposed—frameworks that may very well shield the threat of what can happen if we simply approach each discussion of a work of fiction with wonder and grace.

—Raul Palma,
author of *A Haunting in Hialeah Gardens*

Kasia Bartoszyńska's new treatise on the pleasures of book clubs is a treat: while scholars tend to imagine the hypothetical addressee of a literary work as a solitary figure, Bartoszynska explores what can be learned, and what can be built, from reading in community. In doing so, she reactivates some crucial but undervalued elements of the reader's craft, from the pleasure of hating, to the precision of boredom, with plenty of exuberance and delight along the way. Modeling for her own readers an open-mindedness and curiosity about books that reflects a long time spent in the intellectually immersive and destabilizing space of the humanities classroom, Bartoszyńska takes her own education outside, and shares it with those of us willing to touch grass, and hold hands, in companionable company. The book will delight readers of many kinds.

—Grace Lavery

Reading Together

Katarzyna Bartoszyńska

Ode Books

A collaboration between
the Seminary Co-op Bookstores
and Prickly Paradigm Press
Chicago

Published by Ode Books
Prickly Paradigm Press
5751 S. Woodlawn Avenue, Chicago 60637

www.odebooks.com

ISBN: 9781958846148

Library of Congress Control Number: 2025932916

Printed in the United States of America on acid-free paper.

Reading is often thought of as a solitary activity: readers of Saint Augustine's *Confessions* are as surprised by Augustine's wonder at seeing Ambrose reading silently as Augustine was surprised to be seeing it. And this solitude is generally a delicious one, a private escape from the toils of the surrounding world. But the pleasure of books is, after all, often one of ideas, and ideas blossom when shared (as Fred Moten says: "Is there a way of being intellectual that isn't social?"[1]). The joys of a text multiply in surprising and unexpected ways when you read it with others.

---

1. Stefano Harney and Fred Moten, *The Undercommons: Fugitive Planning and Black Study* (Autonomedia, 2013), 110. This is a good moment to warn you that I love footnotes. This one was just for bibliographic purposes, but I generally embrace the use of paratext for little side conversations. Some people hate that. I don't understand them.

For many people, the only experience they ever have of reading the same book at the same time with a group of other people is in a classroom, and though this can be inspiring and formative, it can also be stultifying and miserable (it was an English class that taught me to appreciate Faulkner's *Light in August*, but it was also an English class that forever ruined any chance I had of enjoying *The Great Gatsby*). Another space of shared reading is in a religious community, but here, similarly to schools, the texts tend to be limited, sometimes even to one. And as often as not, classrooms and religious communities are structured by hierarchies: there is someone in the room who knows more than the others, who has some amount of expertise and perhaps some authority to impose their own interpretation upon everyone else. *This is what you are supposed to notice. This is what the book is* really *saying.*

Enter the book club. Often mocked, derided as an excuse for housewives to gather and drink chardonnay, the book club is the rare space where people come together to discuss shared readings in a totally voluntary way, driven by a desire for community and shared learning. It is grounded in the idealistic assumption that everyone's ideas are worthwhile, that everyone has something to teach and to contribute. Now, to be fair, some clubs are better than others: your mileage may vary.[2] But I have come to believe that the book club is a very specific kind of space, one that opens up a different kind of perspective on books, and produces a particular form of knowledge that you won't encounter elsewhere.

I think about the kinds of knowledge we get from books a lot, you see, because I am an English professor, which means that I spend plenty of time talking about books with various people for whom those conversations are often supposed to be, quite literally, educational. And though I sometimes tell my students that I want our class to be like a really good book club, that's not entirely true—I know full well that it won't be, and I spend a lot of time thinking about why, and considering the differences between my classrooms and my book clubs, and the different kinds of reading that I do.

2. I tell my friend Lauren that I'm writing about how book clubs teach you things, and she narrows her eyes at me and says, "You only think that because you've always been in book clubs with smart people." This is probably true.

I have been in a few different book clubs, some of which, I acknowledge, were really more like classrooms. I have to tell you that being an English professor at a book club session is a little like being a cop at the family cookout—people are slightly nervous about saying the wrong thing around you. They worry that you're judging them, and they think you know the "right" answer. It's embarrassing. And sometimes, they actually just want you to teach them—after all, don't people pay thousands of dollars for the privilege of being in your classrooms?

This is particularly true of the book club that I helped facilitate at a prison in rural Illinois for a group of men serving long-term sentences. They were hungry for knowledge, eager to be educated, and here I was, an "expert." I, likely as a result of various terrible movies, had expected them to be skeptical about the merits of fiction, difficult to persuade—and admittedly, sometimes they were. But I had not really understood how blatantly that space would be crisscrossed by various power hierarchies—the most obvious being that they were prisoners, and I was free. I was a highly educated college professor, in a respectable and honored profession,[3] while they were cast out of society, reviled. But though they might have seen our meetings as being more like classes, I tried very hard not to.

People ask me, often enough that I realize many are probably wondering but not asking: "Were you scared at the prison?" And truly: not really. I'm generally nervous when teaching—anxious that I'll say something stupid, or something that upsets people; that the discussion won't go anywhere; that people will be bored or stop listening; or worse, that they will start chatting among themselves and ignoring me altogether. When I was teaching at Bilkent University, in Ankara, Turkey, I would occasionally have to be a disciplinarian, sternly demanding that the class pay attention. "You seem to be having your own discussion. Would you like to share with the class?" Once I kicked two students out of the

---

3. Seemingly. They certainly appeared to think so, which surprised me somewhat. I don't think of teachers as being particularly well regarded in the United States, and tend to assume that college professors are considered to be at best out-of-touch eggheads or wannabe revolutionaries, but more likely, elitist scum. My experiences teaching in Turkey, where teaching truly *is* considered a noble profession, only strengthened this view.

room, injected some anger into my voice and told them to leave. A flex. Even though I generally tell my students to call me Kasia, we all know that I'm the one in charge. The stakes are a little higher in a prison; the threat of losing control of the room seems more serious. But for the participants too—our little program was tenuous, after all. They had to be on their best behavior or they'd lose access to this privilege, which was at very least something different to do for a few hours every week. I was never afraid that they'd hurt me, which is, I assume, what people really mean when they ask.[4]

But back to the point—although the men in that prison might have seen me as knowing all kinds of things that they didn't, about books but perhaps also about the world, I knew that they know things that I don't. Things that I have only read about in books, or seen in bad movies, that I am hopelessly naïve about. They know things about human nature and society that I do not allow myself to know, though they are

4. Perhaps this was naïve of me. Preti Taneja's *Aftermath* (Transit Books, 2021) is a stunning work that grapples with, and mourns, such harm, and crucially, insists that we also recognize that prisons are a manifestation of state violence.

exactly the kinds of things that so many of the books I teach purport to be interested in: struggle, desperation, cruelty. The awful things that humans can do to each other and the murky ways that structural forces impact individuals, meld with desire, rage, determination.

I'm not trying to romanticize or essentialize that difference between them and me. It is simply a fact that although my upbringing was more cosmopolitan than many, it was also relatively sheltered,[5] and everything in my socialization as a middle-class, highly educated white woman has worked to instill in me a profound ignorance of what it is like to be locked up in a literal prison, not to mention what it is like to grow up poor[6] and uneducated, as many of

5. Nobody has ever hit me in the face, for instance. I suspect this is a more significant distinction between people than many of the more conventional events that we think of as formative experiences.

6. Or rather, poor with no clear prospect for improvement. As contemporary conversations about student loan payments highlight, plenty of academics (especially those who are contingently employed) are poor in money terms, fighting to pay off debt, living on meager stipends or salaries, struggling to make ends meet. But they are conditioned to see this state as temporary, to believe that they will rise above it eventually. That belief seems, increasingly, to be crumbling.

the men in that group (though not all) had. Indeed, the higher up you go in academia, the more you are siloed into a set of norms, habits, and values, a certain kind of "normalcy." Having come from a family of Polish academics, I found much of that world felt intuitive and comfortable. I was instilled with an unquestioned sense of the importance of research and a deep and abiding love for it; a belief that education matters but is also a pleasure in its own right. Only later did I begin to notice how those norms included a discomfort with, or outright contempt or disgust for, those outside the ivory tower. This disdain pairs readily with an urban-rural divide: the academic is the effete cosmopolitan city dweller, gazing with fascinated horror at the country bumpkin.[7]

---

7. Only later, too, did I realize that universities are far from being enlightened sanctuaries from the ugly bigotries of the outside world: not only are they just as structured by those rigid, exclusionary hierarchies of race and gender, but also, the cult of genius frequently serves to excuse truly appalling behavior and shield wrongdoing from consequence. Recent years have made public the open secret of how common sexual harassment and assault are on college campuses, for instance. Read Seo-Young Chu's devastating essay, "A Refuge for Jae-in Doe: Fugues in the Key of English Major" for an example. (*CUNY Academic Works*, November 2017, https://academicworks.cuny.edu/qc_pubs/503/).

I say this to explain that coming to central Illinois for a job in an English department at a small liberal arts college was also a shock of sorts. Here was a school in the middle of the cornfields, far from the pleasures of city life. Here were people who mostly valued teaching above research. Here were people who were devoutly religious, openly so. I like to think that I was not an elitist urban dirtbag, but I was certainly a fish out of water. My point is: though there was a clear distance between me and the men in that prison, there were many things about the lives of the women in another book club of mine, composed of faculty and staff members at the college, ages ranging from thirties to fifties, that were similarly alien. I had read Marilynne Robinson's *Gilead*, and Jane Smiley's *Thousand Acres*, and Kent Haruf's *Our Souls at Night*; I had some ideas about what this life in a smaller, rural area might be like. But what did I know, really?

Here, then, is the tension between theory and practice, between abstract knowledge and embodied experience. Fiction fascinates me in part because it straddles those divides. Novels are made-up stories that attempt to capture and convey particular experiences, but that also construct worlds, help us understand our own world by showing it to us in different ways.

I should mention that I hate the idea of fiction being primarily an empathy machine, a mechanism to put you in someone else's shoes and show you the world from their perspective. This is a very popular idea, especially in recent years, as various articles have purported to explain "Why Reading Books Can Make You a Better Person," backed by scientific studies that breathlessly enthuse over MRIs showing how parts of the brain light up when people pass their eyes over words on a page.[8] I resent this notion (though a part of me also believes it, of course)—there's something so blandly instrumental about it. It's all so pious and dull.

And yet, what I love about my book clubs is precisely the way that they open up other people's lives

---

8. For a nuanced critique of such claims and a broader examination of what happens in your brain when you read, see Paul B. Armstrong, *Stories and the Brain: The Neuroscience of Narrative* (Johns Hopkins University Press, 2020). Tangentially, for a fun and playful book about how we visualize things as we read about them, check out Peter Mendelsund, *What We See When We Read* (Vintage, 2014).

for me, and make me curious about what it was like for them to read the same words I was reading. And their perspectives make me see the books differently—they invite me to try out different ways of reading them.

That is what this book is about: the different ways we read and share ideas, and the unique space that book clubs occupy within that ecosystem. Or rather, the different ways that *I* read, in various groups and spaces, and what that has taught me about books, and reading, and about myself.

As I will explain, literary studies as a discipline has spent plenty of time debating how literary critics read and what the purpose of our scholarship is. I'm interested in those debates, and in the nature of our expertise, but I think many of the claims about the "public humanities" or the relevance of our work are characterized by a fundamental lack of understanding (or curiosity) about how people outside of academia read.

In a book club, I am not in charge of the conversation the way that I am in my classrooms. Because the secret truth is that although all of my classes are discussion-based, and I invite my students to contribute their own ideas or raise issues that interest them, there's always an agenda, a shadow itinerary charting the course of our conversation. I am delighted by tangents and meanderings and alternate routes, but we are nonetheless wandering in a park with a few well-trodden footpaths and a clear list of sights to see. I am the tour guide.

In a book club, I'm the tourist. I try not to be that really annoying tourist who feels a need to show off how much they know about the sites we're visiting; to really just relax and see things with new eyes, maybe do a little off-roading. And in the process, to understand different ways of seeing this place. That's what I want to think through a little more, here—the kind of knowledge about books that book clubs make possible. The kind that comes from something that isn't quite the critical reading you learn in a classroom, or at least in my classroom.

But there's a complication, a plot twist. The more I try to think about how my book clubs are different from my classes, the more the two seem to blur into each other. It doesn't help that more recently, in some of my book clubs, I *am* supposed to be in charge of the conversation, at least somewhat. This was true at the prison, maybe more so than I was willing to admit to myself at the time, but it is even more obviously true lately. About a year ago, I took over as discussion leader for a book club, a job that a friend of mine had been doing, for pay, for almost twenty years. And there's the antiracist learning group that I've been cofacilitating, which also hovers somewhere between a class and a study group—another one of these spaces where I am not exactly teaching, but am nonetheless in some sense responsible for the quality of the discussion. That our conversations are often about the various and subtle ways that power is manifested and reinforced in social interactions only makes this blurring more vertiginous. These are both arenas of shared reading and discussion that aren't exactly classrooms, but where the conversations aren't really *for* me: I'm there for everyone else.

I sense that my teaching is changing too, responding to the changes in my students (and myself) in recent years, and to a shifting social reality: the post-pandemic world, the "crisis in the humanities," the conversations about equity and inclusion spurred by the #BlackLivesMatter and #MeToo movements (and the fears of "wokeness" and "cancel culture" promulgated in response to them), the rise of ChatGPT. As I increasingly come to question the conventions tacitly assumed to signal academic rigor, I am forced to grapple in very pragmatic ways with the question of what I am actually requiring of my students and what I want them to learn—how I am teaching them to read.

Writing this is uncomfortable, because I am doubly exposed—on the one hand, as an academic writing about my personal life, and on the other hand, as an academic writing about my pedagogy. This, then, is an assay—a test of my own theories of reading, and an account of how being in book clubs has changed me, and an examination of different ways of reading together (with some discussion of a handful of books). I indulge in the contemporary fashion of thinking through fragments, or vignettes,[9] because it makes

9. An especially wonderful example is *This Little Art*, by Kate Briggs (Fitzcarraldo Editions, 2017).

sense to me; it's how my mind works (especially these days). But I don't intend to evade the labor of connecting them into some kind of whole, though I do hope that you will join me in the effort.

Reading Jordy Rosenberg's *Confessions of the Fox* made me feel exposed in all kinds of ways. The novel is a sort of mystery thriller, a story within a story about a professor who discovers a manuscript, the confessions of the eighteenth-century English thief Jack Sheppard. The manuscript describes Jack's adventures, and his love affair with a woman named Bess. But what especially intrigues the professor, a trans man, is that it reveals that Jack was assigned female at birth and that Bess is a woman of color. "So then, between this characterization [of Bess] and that of Jack's assigned sex, what we have here is either the most or least authentic Sheppard document in existence."[10]

Like many an eighteenth-century novel, *Confessions of the Fox* begins with a fictional note

10. Jordy Rosenberg, *Confessions of the Fox: A Novel* (One World, 2018), 27.

from an editor, the professor, before proceeding to the manuscript, Jack's tale. The professor provides explanatory footnotes to the story that gradually take on a life of their own, stretching from one page to another, becoming a space to meditate on the uniqueness of the manuscript and also to tell his own story, to chronicle his various problems with the university's administration and in his dating life.

The uniqueness of the novel is not only its postmodern flourishes of interweaving two tales, two moments in time, through clever uses of footnotes—but also that those footnotes firmly ground the study of the manuscript in the real-life scholarship of eighteenth-century studies, providing references and brief glosses of theoretical arguments. It is the version of eighteenth-century studies that I know and love, and feel most connected to—the one that offers thrilling, innovative examinations of concepts of race and gender and bodies that were beginning to crystallize at that time, in the period we used to think of as the Enlightenment, but that were also still open, experimental, as too were the forms of the texts (which is to say: what appear to be the novel's "post-modern" flourishes are actually very very eighteenth century).

In other words, this is a novel for which I am the ideal audience: someone who knows the scholarship and can appreciate the brilliance of the text's playfulness. It feels almost like an inside joke, it is so deeply interwoven with the scholarly things that I think about for work and assume no one else cares about or finds interesting. Would other people enjoy it? Would they find it too weird, too dry, too academic? I felt possessive—*This book is for ME! I understand it and appreciate it in ways that none of you can!* (observe here the way appreciation feels proprietary, like knowledge, like expertise).

I read it with my book club of women working at the same small college in Illinois, some of whom were professors (others were staff in various administrative positions, and one was the chaplain), but none in literary studies. They all enjoyed the book. They were pleased and amused to learn that the texts referred to in the footnotes were real, and although they were probably most interested in the question of whether the main character was an actual historical person, they were interested to hear that the issues raised in the notes are real topics of study in eighteenth-century literature.

One of the powerful things that the novel does is to raise the question of how we think, and write, about nonconforming gender identity in the past—but also in the present. Jodie[11] was particularly struck by the series of footnotes that invited reflection on what exactly we needed to know about Jack's body. In the first sex scene between Jack and Bess, the editor observes that it is "Remarkable that Jack's genitalia are not described in detail. Unlike almost any other sexological or protosexological document from the period (and after), which exfoliate layer after layer of prurient fantasies about the sex organs,"[12] and goes on to list examples of such documents (which are, of course, real). A few pages later, another scene of lovemaking, and the editor reappears: "In what can

11. Yes, I have invented pseudonyms for some of the people I talk about.
12. Rosenberg, 92.

only be described as gallantry, the speaker declines to showcase Bess' body for the reader. Incidentally: a much better boyfriend than I ever was."[13] And then on the next page: "It is almost certain that if there were a hack job this section would include a voyeuristic depiction of Jack's genitalia. I consider this elegant declining-to-describe to be strong evidence of the text's authenticity. Of course, personally, I'm more than happy to go on at length about my prodigious genitalia. But there's a difference between a confession one wants to give, and one that is taken."[14]

These notes ask us to think about privacy, consent, vulnerability, curiosity, desire. But they do not tell us, exactly—they do not scold. They invite us to identify with the position that articulates the critique of the prurient gaze, even as they extend a kind of grace by observing how the narrator himself fails to live up to this standard. And of course, our curiosity is not entirely prurient: information is the basis of knowledge. If we want to know about people's lives in the past, we must go beneath the public

---

13. Rosenberg, 108.
14. Rosenberg, 109.

surface—we must know Jack's secret. This tension between an impulse to shelter vulnerable people in the past from prying eyes and the hunger to know more about their most intimate experiences is a core problem in the history of marginalized people. In a few footnotes, *Confessions of the Fox* invites you into this scholarly debate.[15]

My fellow book club members didn't really care if the scholarship was real; they enjoyed the story and the clever structure. *Is this what it means to be an academic, to care about the scholarly apparatus?* I wondered. The point was, they learned stuff! But so did I—a very basic thing, but it felt somewhat revelatory nonetheless, which is that people actually do find the things that I study for a living interesting. English professors have a minority complex, coming in part from

---

15. Readers who are interested in some approachable scholarly works that take up this problem are warmly invited to read Wendy Anne Warren, "'The Cause of Her Grief': The Rape of a Slave in Early New England," *The Journal of American History* 93, no. 4 (March 2007), 1031–1049; Saidiya Hartman, "Venus in Two Acts," *Small Axe* 12, no. 2 (June 2008), 1–14; and Susan Stryker, "(De)Subjugated Knowledges: An Introduction to Transgender Studies," in *The Transgender Studies Reader*, ed. Susan Stryker and Stephen Whittle (Routledge, 2006), 1–18. For a more public-facing example of hybrid history writing, see other work by Hartman, especially *Wayward Lives, Beautiful Experiments*.

all the jokes we hear about the English major barista and the articles about English being the major people most regret, the one promising the lowest salary after graduation (though there is in fact plenty of evidence to suggest the opposite[16]). That this sense of our own irrelevance is so deep-seated shows how economic conditions really do shape your life in all kinds of ways.

But as you might have noticed, I was still reading the book, and engaging in the conversation, as an academic—I couldn't quite shake my critical distance. The novel's open invitation to notice that distance and think about how academics read was too irresistible for academic analysis—I couldn't get out of my own way. I still feel like I missed something in that conversation with my book club; I couldn't get free of my own head enough.

Maybe it's that thing, the one that I missed, that I'm chasing here.

---

16. See, for instance, David Deming, "In the Salary Race, Engineers Sprint but English Majors Endure," *The New York Times*, September 20, 2019, or "Report on English Majors' Career Preparation and Outcomes," MLA Association of Departments of English, March 13, 2024, https://www.maps.mla.org/Resources/Reports-and-Other-Resources/Report-on-English-Majors-Career-Preparation-and-Outcomes.

Perhaps it's my imposter syndrome speaking, but I'm somewhat resistant to the idea that my own knowledge about whatever text is so vastly superior, that I have the insider scoop as far as the essential things to know about books. I know plenty of things about literary history and the mechanics of texts, yes. I have read lots and lots of books and know a decent amount of history, so I get some of the references, and pick up on connections, or notice when someone is doing something subversive or subtle with form. But I'm not coming to book clubs to hear myself talk. I want to know what everyone else has to say. I want to know what they know about the book that I don't.

This may be surprising. It would seem that the whole point of getting a PhD in literature is to know more about books than other people do, and it is true that much of our profession is based on the assumption that other people don't know how to read—a dismissal and lack of curiosity about how others interact with books. Michael Warner opens a wonderful essay on this phenomenon musing, "Students who come to my literature classes, I find, read in all the ways they aren't supposed to."[17] "My work is cut out for me," he says—he is supposed to teach them critical reading, which is different from "all these modes of their actual reading" that would instead be termed uncritical.[18]

Warner's essay elegantly pursues the question of what, exactly, is this thing called "critical reading," and why it is so hard to define. *How do we know that we are actually teaching it if we can't even define it?* you may be wondering. As he notes, while we do not entirely know what critical reading is, we know how to do it—the set of techniques or practices that it comprises.

The question of what critical or close reading really is fascinates me, of course, but at the moment my interest lies elsewhere: I'm after a more textured account of "uncritical" reading, or at least one version of it. As Warner notes, uncritical reading

---

17. Michael Warner, "Uncritical Reading," in *Polemic: Critical or Uncritical*, ed. Jane Gallop (Routledge, 2004), 13–38.
18. Warner, 13.

is arguably "the unconscious of our profession"—the thing we are always responding to, managing, controlling. The worlds organized around such reading, he says, are terra incognita.[19] Some of those unknown worlds have since been at least partially mapped.[20] But, to my knowledge at least, book clubs are comparatively unexplored, though even a cursory internet search will turn up tips for making yours better, and novels increasingly come packaged with supplementary questions for discussion at the end, which suggests a method, if not a theory, of what book clubs do.

It is my contention that book clubs can produce a unique form of reading, a different kind of attention, as an ongoing practice of examining books that is meaningfully different from what takes place in classrooms—a difference in kind, and not only degree. Because the conversation is different, so too is the knowledge that it produces, and over time, this also

---

19. Warner, 33.
20. *Paraliterary: The Making of Bad Readers in Postwar America*, by Merve Emre (University of Chicago Press, 2017) is one example; Tim Aubry, *Reading as Therapy: What Contemporary Fiction Does for Middle-Class Americans* (University of Iowa Press, 2011) is another.

shapes the way people read, the things they notice as they anticipate those conversations.

Most obviously, book clubs turn reading into a communal experience, opening up an interpersonal dimension that changes your perspective. If you know that you'll be talking to your friend Rosalia about Quan Barry's *We Ride Upon Sticks*, and you know that Rosalia was herself on a hockey team in high school, you will inevitably wonder, *Will she see herself in this story? Is this what her experience was like?* If a detail strikes you as unlikely or strange, you might remind yourself to ask her about it. You won't be seeing through her eyes, exactly, but you'll be thinking about the book in part through your relationship to Rosalia. And here's the cool part: you'll arrive at the club meeting, and Rosalia will have noticed all kinds of things that you completely missed (because you weren't seeing through her eyes at all, even if you tried to), but you'll ask her your questions anyhow, and she'll sit back and press her lips together and furrow her brow slightly, in that way she does, and go, "Hmmm, I didn't think about that," or maybe she'll give a little start of excitement and go, "Oh! That's interesting!" but actually, her take on that scene was totally different, it reminded her of this other friend she had in high school, and the pizza place they'd go to… And you will learn something new about Rosalia, and maybe about pizza, and also about *We Ride Upon Sticks*.

I did not much like Otessa Moshfegh's *My Year of Rest and Relaxation*. A big reason was that I was just so, so annoyed by the final two pages, the clumsy tie-in to 9/11 that felt utterly gratuitous and distracting. There's an argument to be made that it changes the sense of scale, that it's intended to make you think about how much the narrator's suffering "matters" in light of this other tragedy. Fine. I hated it.

Mostly, I was just kind of bored by the book. It was sort of interesting conceptually, but it went on and on, and I just didn't care all that much. What did vaguely pique my interest was wondering what the other women in the book club would think. How would they respond to this fairly salacious story of casual sex and prolific drug use? I was pretty sure that most of them had never done any serious partying. Would they find it shocking? Would they relish the vicarious experience of taboo pleasures (I was sure that at least one of them would), or would this just be further evidence that drug use is both cause and symptom of pathology?

Let me pause here to note that many seemingly straitlaced Midwestern folk probably have much more colorful pasts than you realize. One of the most delightfully wild women I knew in my mid-twenties, who gigglingly confessed to me that when she went on the farm visit that was part of her wholesome organic CSA, she ended up having a threesome with two of the farmhands in a barn; indeed, who guilelessly seduced me after a night of drinking and dancing, ended up quitting our entire social circle to devote herself to a man so Christian that he wouldn't have sex before marriage. Sometimes I look her up on Facebook, and there are cheerful comment threads from her fellow church members enthusing about her trio of charming children. You would never have guessed.

So it was possible, I thought, that the book club ladies would have some stories to tell, and I was very much hoping to hear them—I love a salacious yarn. And I was fully willing to share a few of my own, to help them along.

But we didn't talk about that stuff at all. In fact, people had noticed all kinds of things that I hadn't, or hadn't paid attention to. Ann kept returning us to the question of grief and mourning, noting the narrator's various references to her mother's death. She talked about her own experience of grief, and how she identified so strongly with the way that the narrator kept insisting that it wasn't the point, and yet, it so clearly was; it kept popping up at the most unexpected moments. This was a revelation to me. She was so right—the narrator's grief was like a tectonic plate upon which the entire story was perched, occasionally sending tremors through the rest.

As we spoke, a question occurred to me. One of the people in the book club is an artist, whose work is conceptual but also quite material—she makes actual pieces of art, paintings and collages and sculptures, physical things that are beautiful. What did she think about the way that art was represented in the novel? This spurred another thought: What if we thought of the novel itself as a form of conceptual art; in what ways is it similar to the kinds of artworks it describes? But mostly, I wanted to hear about how Stephanie thought about art, something I had never thought to ask her.

I learned new things about my friends that day, not in the prurient way that I was anticipating, but through a deeper understanding of some aspects of their lives and worldviews that also, unexpectedly, gave me a completely different perspective on *My Year of Rest and Relaxation*. I still wouldn't recommend the book to anyone, but I very much recommend the conversation I had about it with those women; it was fantastic.

There is a secret fear haunting this little assay of mine. I have been telling you that I frequently (though less and less so) question my own expertise in literature, and arguing for the benefits of a kind of reading that is not valorized by academia, a particular form of uncritical reading that I am claiming book clubs can inculcate. But I am plagued by another kind of worry, which is whether I am helplessly trapped in my own way of (critical) reading—whether I can actually access the kinds of pleasure and knowledge that I am advocating for.[21] Have I been so thoroughly trained in my discipline that I am unable to read in any other way? Am I trapped behind a wall of critical distance and abstraction, unable to inhabit the text in the way that nonacademic readers do, or to ask the sorts of questions they raise?

But does uncritical reading actually require me to shed my knowledge and skills, my habits of reading? Or is it something else that I'm after—a different kind of conversation?

21. Not that the kind of reading that I do doesn't give me pleasure—it does, very much so. But perhaps of a different kind?

I don't know the actual history of book clubs. It should be noted that there are different kinds that emerge for different purposes—the classic example, to me, is the consciousness-raising group. I am always deeply moved, reading the Combahee River Collective statement, by the part about how "Black feminists often talk about their feelings of craziness before becoming conscious of the concepts of sexual politics, patriarchal rule, and most importantly, feminism, the political analysis and practice that we women use to struggle against oppression."[22] And then, as their work progresses, their decision to form a study group, to share not only their reading but also their writing, and subsequently, to pursue publication for a wider audience. How incredible, that this profound work of feminist thought came out of these conversations!

Academia is often characterized as the solitary pursuit of a lone genius, but this to me is the more inspiring genesis of theory—a group of women reading and talking together, writing for one another.

---

22. Keeanga-Yamahtta Taylor, ed., *How We Get Free: Black Feminism and the Combahee River Collective* (Haymarket Books, 2017), 17.

A space where the personal, practical, and theoretical collide, where women share their experiences, confirm *This isn't just me, right?* and strategize to create resources for themselves and for others.[23]

I'm not saying that every book club is a consciousness-raising group, but even if they are intended for recreation and pleasure, I think there's inevitably some kind of collective work that happens when people come together to discuss a text.

When we think about the kind of reading that happens outside of schools, ironically, one of the first

23. For example: "We discovered that all of us, because we were 'smart,' had also been considered 'ugly,' i.e., 'smart ugly.' 'Smart-ugly' crystallized the way in which most of us had been forced to develop our intellects at great cost to our 'social' lives." (Taylor, 20–21) Sara Ahmed describes the genesis of theory, especially feminist theory, in similar ways. Writing about what she calls "sweaty concepts," she says: "Feminist ideas are what we come up with to make sense of what persists. We have to persist in or by coming up with feminist ideas. Already in this idea is a different idea about ideas. Ideas would not be something generating through distance, a way of abstracting something from something, but from our involvement in a world that often leaves us, frankly, bewildered (…) too often conceptual work is understood as distinct from describing a situation" (12–13). Sara Ahmed, *Living a Feminist Life* [Duke University Press, 2017], 12–13.

things that springs to mind is reading for instruction or wisdom, treating texts as religious guidance or self-help books. I imbibed an unconscious disdain for such writing fairly early in life, until someone gave me a copy of *How to Write a Journal Article in 20 Weeks*. The opening chapter, on writer's block, was revelatory. What a relief, to have one's problems so clearly diagnosed, and the approach to managing them so straightforwardly presented![24] And then I became a mother and discovered the world of parenting guides. Millennials on social media often joke that they need a manual for life. Parents, it turns out, are awash in them. Of course, these guides are frequently contradictory, even as they are adamant that if you do not follow their instructions to the letter, your child will never sleep in their own room for the entire night.[25]

---

24. This turned out to be my gateway into reading various guides to writing. The best I've found so far is *Write No Matter What! Advice for Academics* by Joli Jensen (University of Chicago Press, 2017), though *The Artist's Way: A Spiritual Path to Higher Creativity*, by Julia Cameron (Tarcher, 2016), is also kind of life-changing, if you can tolerate the kookiness. I can say with all honesty that if it weren't for these various books, you probably wouldn't be reading this now.

25. Admittedly, mine still regularly climbs into bed with us in the wee morning hours, so I have obviously failed to heed the correct advice.

These contradictions force you into a level of critical reflection, demanding that you either choose one book to pledge your faith to or synthesize the competing accounts into some kind of individual theory of your own.

My point is, even reading for instruction isn't that simple.

We had been discussing Richard Dawkins's *Selfish Gene* for over an hour before Ray homed in on the real point of reading the damn thing. I was a ride-along on the discussion—we were required to teach in pairs at the prison, but also, this session came out of the guys requesting to read a science book with our biologist. So I tagged along to learn something myself, the dutiful humanist deferring to the wisdom of science.

I struggled with the book somewhat—it was boring, and more than a little polemical. Knowing a thing or two about Dawkins as a person, I was also resistant from the get-go, primed to disagree. This isn't necessarily a problem, in my field—literary criticism can occasionally be thinly veiled attack.[26] The problem was that I don't have the scientific expertise to meaningfully disagree with Dawkins, and had to defer to the authority of others. This is the challenge of reading nonfiction, and especially, of teaching nonfiction: I can dissect how the argument works or find inconsistencies within it, but otherwise, I have no ground to stand on. So I don't quite know how to engage. And what do we discuss?

But there was another challenge. To me, one of the most interesting aspects of the book is that it's where Dawkins coins the idea of meme, which obviously has taken on a life of its own. And so the question that I wanted to ask was whether his book is actually far more useful in describing internet culture than human biology, and how we could use it to think about the differences between human

26. Some have argued that this is a central problem in literary studies and advocated for different ways of reading; for example, Lisa Ruddick, "When Nothing Is Cool," *The Point Magazine*, December 7, 2015, https://thepointmag.com/criticism/when-nothing-is-cool/, or Rita Felski, *Hooked: Art and Attachment* (University of Chicago Press, 2020). I have to say though, that their descriptions of literary studies seem very different from what I've experienced. But I might be an anomaly (my imposter syndrome whispers other unflattering possibilities).

physical ecologies and the digital world, the problem of analogizing the two, etc. The thing was, a lot of the guys had gotten locked up before the internet emerged—around the time Dawkins was writing the book, actually. And even if they hadn't, it seemed sort of rude to discuss the internet with them when they weren't allowed to access it.

So I wasn't sure what we were going to talk about. And for quite a while, it seemed like we were just going into classroom mode, with the biology professor explaining what Dawkins was saying, until Ray finally asked the real question, the one that rocketed my understanding of the book into an entirely new dimension: "So are the X-men possible or not?"

We have, as a culture, a tendency to instrumentalize our pleasures, to ask what they are good for. If we aren't reading fiction for information, what are we getting out of it?

I mentioned already the idea that fiction trains you in empathy. This isn't so far from the classic notion of the canon, the Great Books that are meant to teach you to be a Great Human Being. It is notable that the process seems to operate in only one direction, toward betterment—rarely are concerns voiced that Dostoevsky might actually inspire readers to homicide[27] (then again, book banning has been making a comeback). But whereas literature departments, when called upon to articulate their own value in a time of shrinking budgets, will reach for more ambiguous benefits like "enhanced critical thinking skills," popular media tend to be far more lofty in their claims for the benefits of reading. It's not hard to find lists of books you *must* read before you die, books that will make you a better person, that will make you a Real Man, etc.

Of course I believe that books teach you things and make you think differently. But I am pretty firmly opposed to the idea that anyone can clearly predict what those things are. The longer I've been teaching, in fact, the more I feel like I have no idea

---

27. Josh Landy summarizes these various arguments, and the problems with them, in *How to Do Things with Fictions* (Oxford University Press, 2014).

what my students will ultimately take from the experience of being in my classroom. Increasingly, my final paper assignments are loose reflections, asking them to tell me about something, anything, they learned (or to explain why they didn't learn anything), and the results are revelatory. But I also know that they don't really know yet—they'll only find out in years to come. I actually suspect that more often, what happens is a fairly mortifying moment where you realize, in your thirties, say, how deeply wrong you were about something, cringing to think of the impassioned proclamations you made in class, and you recall, hazily, how the teacher had in fact gently tried to suggest another way of thinking. At least, I hope I'm not the only one who experienced that. But anyway, my point is, most of the grand claims about the benefits of books fill me with skepticism.

However, I will defend some aspects of these exalted claims. Another version of the argument for certain kinds of reading, these days, is the injunction to diversify your reading list, which implicitly suggests that reading books by and about people who are different from you will make you less racist. I hasten to say that although I feel a contrarian resentment of many instrumental arguments about empathy and moral edification, and a significant degree of skepticism about the extent to which fiction teaches antiracism,[28] I also think that reading diversely is an obvious good. And reading literature in translation is a necessary corrective to the staggering provincialism of American exceptionalism. It's also just more interesting, honestly. Aren't you curious?

And I do think that people should read fiction. I mean really, everyone. But it's hard for me to explain why.

When I first started volunteering at the prison, it was in a program for people who were soon to be released, and we were tasked with designing a curriculum that would help the men develop some skills that would be

28. In the antiracist workshop for which I help design the curriculum, we don't read any fiction.

useful in the outside world. This was supposed to be things like how to interview for a job, how to budget responsibly, etc., but our unit ended up being about something that got defined as "emotional intelligence" and was centered around empathy (the irony of me codesigning such a thing, I know). I really just wanted an excuse to get everyone a copy of Walter Mosley's *Always Outnumbered, Always Outgunned*, because I love the book, and because I suspected that they would be surprised to find that someone was writing literary fiction about the day-to-day struggles of a newly released inmate.

This is the constant refrain in the argument for diversifying curriculums and reading lists, and it is more persuasive than the idea that fiction can teach you about people who are different from you—the primal scene of someone's delighted surprise to see themselves in a book they have been assigned. To be seen by the world of books deemed worthy of reading in a classroom.

I have my own version of this story, of course. In a college class on autobiography that I took with Roger

Porter, we read Eva Hoffman's *Lost in Translation*, the autobiography of a Polish Jewish woman whose family moved to Canada when she was a kid. She describes registering for school, and how her little sister's name was changed from Alina to Elaine,[29] and suddenly I remembered being in some kind of office at Pierce Park Elementary school in Boise, Idaho, where I was going to start fourth grade among children who had mostly been born not only in the same town but even in the same hospital ("because St. Al's doesn't deliver babies"), quite a jolting contrast to my first four years of schooling in Berkeley, California, where the curriculum regularly featured parents of classmates coming in to give minilessons about their home culture and treating us to samples of their local foods. Now, in Idaho, some school official was suggesting that I be called Kathy instead of Kasia, and I was shocked. I was NOT a Kathy, or a Katie, or even a Katrina.

It is a curious thing, that I have always identified as Polish and never as American, or even Polish American. Is that because of those first four years in

29. Eva Hoffman, *Lost in Translation: A Life in a New Language* (Penguin, 1989), 105.

Berkeley, where each of my friends was from a different country, so I was naturally linked to Poland, even as my Polish language skills were fading? Or was it rather the first few years in Boise, where I felt like a perpetual outsider, with my classmates constantly asking, "Where are you from?" and then, inevitably, "Poland, where's that?" that cemented in me a sense that I would never be American? Would it have been different if I had become Kathy that day instead of remaining Kasia (not even Katarzyna!), doomed to forever correct people's pronunciation (or, maybe worse, to not even bother correcting it)?

What I identified with, reading Hoffman, was not so much the painful experiences of struggling to assimilate—though I did find in those scenes something that seemed like it could be a retroactive explanation of my constant failure to fit in, a more appealing one, maybe, than the idea that I might just be weird, antisocial, or prickly—but her account of dual identity, being between languages, cultures, worlds. At the end of the book, she writes, "When I speak Polish now, it is infiltrated, permeated, and inflected by the English in my head. Each language modifies the other, crossbreeds with it, fertilizes it. Each language makes the other relative. Like everybody, I am the sum of my languages—the language of my family and childhood, and education and friendship, and love, and the larger, changing world—though perhaps I tend to be more aware than most of the fractures between them, and of the building blocks."[30] This was the guide I needed to help me understand the various parts of myself in relation to one another, the disjointedness of my life narrative in comparison to those of other people I knew. A way to think about my identity outside of absolutes and illusions of ethnic purity and authenticity that I would never be able to attain anyhow. It was also, no doubt, a crucial gateway into my love of formalism in literary studies—an approach to texts that considers how they are constructed and how the different pieces, and the interactions between them, create meaning.

It wasn't that I had previously thought that my life was unworthy of being represented in literature, or

---

30. Hoffman, 273.

that I had struggled to identify with the people I'd been reading about (I had deeply felt the pangs of being an orphan, a pirate, a musketeer, a Shoshoni girl on the run, etc., with no difficulty). But it really is astonishing when a book represents something that is intimately familiar to you, and that you know is foreign to many people you know. It reconstellates your relationship to the world, and to books, and to yourself.

But it would be a fool's errand to try to design a course where everyone would encounter their own experience reflected in the books they read. And I didn't assume that Mosley's novel would do that for the guys in our program, necessarily, but I did want to present them with something that might seem more directly relevant to their own experiences, without having an obvious and explicit moral. This was in a sense contradictory to the aims of the program, which was supposed to have a clear agenda and to teach identifiable skills. So those mainstream arguments about empathy were a convenient justification that allowed me to essentially just share a book that I thought they'd find engaging.

And despite my qualms about my own qualifications to teach anyone life skills, the program did seem to be somewhat successful. But it also highlighted the fact that there was little to no programming available to those who were more controversial recipients of such goodwill, from society's perspective: people serving long-term sentences for violent or sex crimes. So we started a book club for them. This time there was no particular agenda, no skills that needed to be taught. It was just an opportunity to read together and talk about books. Which, paradoxically, made me think a lot harder about what the point of reading various books was.

I realized very quickly into the Kafka discussion with the guys that my appreciation for that text draws pretty heavily on a fairly significant scholarly apparatus. This was startling to me because in many ways, Kafka's works, though strange and puzzling, are quite approachable—I read plenty of them as a teenager and was enthralled. The setup of *The Metamorphosis*—man transforms into vermin[31]—is immediately vivid and interesting; it's what Kafka does with it that continuously surprises us. And the more we delve into that surprise, the more we are pushed to consider that the book must be doing something else, must be making meaning in some other way, and it is our task to understand how.

This is precisely the work of literary interpretation, of course, so you might expect that Kafka would be the ideal author for persuading people that literary criticism is important. The problem is that the end product of that critical labor is … a bit of a mess.

To my mind, at least. My whole angle on Kafka is that there is no simple answer.[32] Whatever interpretation you come up with, it's never going to completely "work"—there's always a sentence or two in the text that completely mucks it up. So

31. No, not a cockroach. If the opening sentence of your English-language edition contains that word, cross it out. I very much believe that there is no one correct way to translate a text, but there are wrong ones, and that word choice is among the worst of them.

32. This view is derived primarily from a seminar on Kafka I took in college taught by Katja Garloff—one of the best classes I've ever taken. I hope she would not be horrified to hear that this was the lasting mark it left on me, but as mentioned above, you never know, as a teacher, what your students will end up learning. It's entirely possible that this wasn't at all what she sought to impart.

many people read *The Metamorphosis* and come away thinking, "Oh, so this is basically about how capitalism is dehumanizing." I hate this interpretation.[33] The closest I'm willing to go to a firm line on the text is that it invites us to consider what it means to be human by being so puzzlingly unstable.[34]

I thought this would be an excellent discussion to have at the prison. We had already discussed, with great success, both *Frankenstein* and *The Curious Incident of Dr Jekyll and Mr Hyde*, and the guys were very interested in thinking about the idea of the monster, and the problem of evil. *Metamorphosis* seemed like the logical next step.

But Shelley and Stevenson give you a lot more to

33. It was so ubiquitous when I was teaching the text in Turkey that I could spend our first class session on the book making them walk me through the argument for that reading, so that I could demolish it and we could start anew. It's not that hard to do—just focus your attention on the other members of Gregor's family, and the mood at the end, when they all have jobs.

34. This take is largely based on an essay by Stanley Corngold, "Kafka's Metamorphosis: Metamorphosis of the Metaphor," in Franz Kafka, *The Metamorphosis*, ed. and trans. Stanley Corngold (Norton, 1996), 79–106, which argues that the text shows us metamorphosis in process and also illuminates how a metaphor is never fully stable; it can never be a simple substitution of terms. It is probably in my top five favorite works of literary criticism.

work with. Yes, the meanings are multiple, and there's a counterargument to any singular interpretation, but there's at least the illusion that the text wants you to pick one, is telling you something specific. Those other texts seem really to be about how society constructs the idea of a bad person/monster, or drives people to evil, but Kafka's story isn't doing that. Or maybe that's my misreading—it was I who tenaciously refused to let any of their critical readings rest, insisting, "No, it doesn't just say that. Look," I was saying, "look at how it isn't saying any one thing!"

By the end of our two hours, I was questioning myself. *What is the gain in reading this? It's so bizarre, so depressing.* The guys struggled to find some kind of meaning, but every time they suggested an overarching truth that the story revealed, I insisted on finding counterarguments in the text, proving that there couldn't be any one clear takeaway. The story is making you ask the question, yes, but *there is no answer*. In that sense, it is not saying *anything*.

"This is so weird, man," the guys kept saying.

Doesn't seem very satisfying.

Was the conversation constrained by our unwillingness to share too much in the way of personal details? Perhaps. Or to put it differently, maybe we struggled because we stuck a little too closely to the book. In a classroom, you rein in tangents and digressions to stay on task and focused, but in book clubs, there is space to indulge an anecdote or sudden association.

During the pandemic lockdown, some friends and I organized a book club over email, and an edited version of the emails about one of the books we discussed, *Inland*, Téa Obreht's wonderful ghost story set in the American West, was later published online.[35] I have no idea, honestly, if it would be of interest to anyone else, but I still love rereading those emails, and the parts that I love the most, and that sparked new ways of thinking about the book, were moments when someone would bring up connections to something

35. Katarzyna Bartoszyńska, Jennifer Carroll, and Ruchama Johnston-Bloom, "Close Reading at a Distance: Téa Obreht's *Inland*," *ASAP Journal*, October 24, 2020, https://asapjournal.com/close-reading-at-a-distance-tea-obrehts-inland-kasia-bartoszynska-jennifer-j-carroll-and-ruchama-johnston-bloom/.

else they had read or thought about—Ruchama talking about the history of camels, Jen mentioning her friend's work on the Undocumented Migration Project. If one of us was teaching a class on *Inland*, we might include some supplementary readings so that the students could follow our thinking on those aspects of the novel (and maybe take it in other directions)—but that would still be a relatively one-sided conversation. It's in the book club that you open those connections up a bit more, where you can digress more freely and wander into extended personal anecdotes.

I am in a summer seminar on sixteenth- and seventeenth-century Chinese and Japanese fiction, reveling, gloriously, in being a student again. We are discussing *Jin Ping Mei, The Plum in a Golden Vase*, a truly dazzling text. Though it is considered one of the four great classics of Ming dynasty fiction (alongside *Journey to the West*, *Romance of the Three Kingdoms*, and *Dream of the Red Chamber*), it's a controversial novel, absolutely brimming with licentious sex scenes—really hardcore stuff. Scholars wonder: Did people in the seventeenth century actually read the whole thing or just skip to the sex scenes? We tend to assume that pornography is just about erotic stimulation, and that the plot is a pretense, but this is a 3,000-page novel, and there is A LOT of plot. Some theorists take the opposite tack: What if the sex scenes are the spoonful of sugar that helps the medicine go down, the carrot that leads you through the maze of complex (and morally edifying) fiction? We enlightened academics do not require such bribery, of course, and can therefore dismiss such scenes as fluff, merely there to appease the masses.

So this is a real question: Do the sex scenes matter or not? What do they do? Scholars such as Lynn Hunt and Kathleen Lubey have offered compelling arguments that sex scenes in fiction are meaningful in unexpected ways.[36] But you can't discuss this in a classroom without revealing at least a little something about yourself.

---

36. Lynn Hunt, *The Invention of Pornography: Obscenity and the Origins of Modernity, 1500–1800* (Zone Books, 1996); Kathleen Lubey, *What Pornography Knows: Sex and Social Protest Since the Eighteenth Century* (Stanford University Press, 2022).

As we are pondering these questions in the seminar, one of my classmates says, "But isn't this basically like *50 Shades of Grey*—not that I've read it!—a depiction of BDSM to thrill readers who are unlikely to be having these kinds of sexual experiences?"

At this moment, I learn something about myself, which is that I will react strongly when someone characterizes *50 Shades of Grey* as BDSM. It is very important to me that people understand that erotic pain play is not about letting someone hurt you because it gets them off. I want them to know that BDSM involves trust and communication and consent. Not just because I don't want them to think of people in the kink community as deranged freaks, but also because I want them to have the opportunity to explore their own desires in an enjoyable way, and *50 Shades* is not a good model for that. (Admittedly, I haven't actually read it or seen the movie, just read articles about them,[37] but I can't say so without seeming like I'm similarly disavowing my willingness

37. A good one is Emma Green, "Consent Isn't Enough: The Troubling Sex of *Fifty Shades*," *The Atlantic*, February 10, 2015.

to read pornographic fiction, so I leave that out.) I say, "Well, it's not exactly BDSM though, right? I mean, it's a caricature. It completely fails to understand how consent works in these situations. So it's more like a fantasy of domination."

There's a ripple of energy in the room, a twitch in the balance. For a brief moment, there's suddenly the possibility that we might actually talk about sex. People shift slightly in their seats. Will we?

No. We are not here to learn about people's proclivities. We're here to think about *Jin Ping Mei*, and what the sex does in that book. People are nervous, giggling, because at any moment, it seems, their own desires might be briefly glimpsed, and indeed, it's difficult to discuss sex without revealing at least some of your beliefs about it—what you consider "normal," for instance, and what you find distasteful. I guess people worry that an ability to discuss anal sex suggests that one has plenty of experience with it, but I am fairly certain that talking and doing are very different things in this arena, just as I am certain that one's sexual fantasies are not necessarily things one would actually do, or even want to do.[38]

There is a lot of anxiety, especially these days, about how to discuss sex in classroom settings, and for very good reasons. In an undergraduate class especially, the cost-benefit ratio of opening the door for people to share their own sexual experiences does not often work out favorably, and doing so is more likely to derail class discussion of a text than to help anyone understand it.[39]

But in a book club, you actually could have those conversations about the sex people were having or had tried, and I am certain that doing so would also give you a whole new insight into *Jin Ping Mei*.

---

38. I teach Judith Butler's "Imitation and Gender Insubordination" every year, and one of the parts that most blows people's minds is the bit about how "There are no direct expressive or causal lines between sex, gender, gender presentation, sexual practice, fantasy, and sexuality. None of those terms captures or defines the rest." Judith Butler, "Imitation and Gender Insubordination," in *The Lesbian and Gay Studies Reader*, ed. Henry Abelove, Michèle Aina Barale, and David M. Halperin (Routledge, 1993), 315. Another text hugely influential to my thinking about sexual fantasy versus sexual practice is Judith Levine's *Harmful to Minors: The Perils of Protecting Children from Sex* (University of Minnesota Press, 2002).
39. Or maybe better to say that I don't know how to facilitate such conversations effectively. But I know that there are other teachers who do, and their students are lucky people.

Of course, it depends on your book club, and how well you know one another. But it's a context where intimacy forms naturally, and at least some amount of disclosure seems appropriate, if not required. Discussing Annie Ernaux's *Simple Passion*, a brief chronicle of an intense sexual affair, with what I will call my book club of big-city women, all of whom are over sixty, we rather naturally, I think, found ourselves volunteering information about whether we had ever experienced this kind of obsession, and pondering whether we would want to. The point was not to share those stories, but more interestingly, to reflect on whether such a thing could indeed happen to anyone, as Ernaux claims in what to me is one of the most tantalizing passages in the entire book:

> Thanks to him, I was able to approach the frontier separating me from others, to the extent of actually believing that I could sometimes cross it … I discovered what other people are capable of, in other words, anything: sublime

> or deadly desires, lack of dignity, attitudes and beliefs I had found absurd in others until I myself turned to them. Without knowing it, he brought me closer to the world.[40]

To read this book and condemn Ernaux and say to yourself, *This could never happen to me, I would never do this*, is to miss her point that she is not "that kind of person" either. A few of the big-city women were initially dubious about the book (as was I), but this turn at the end was persuasive, perhaps even more so because Ernaux didn't belabor the point and do a lot of work to convince you.

The real skepticism, as it turned out, was not about her behavior with this lover but about her writing. Ernaux explains that she feels no shame writing down the thoughts that compose the book

---

40. Annie Ernaux, *Simple Passion*, trans. Tanya Leslie (Seven Stories Press, 1993), 37. This passage made perfect sense to me, because I had a similar experience when I became a parent: in the very moments where I was a stranger to myself, I found that I had a new connection to the world. Not, as you might imagine, by virtue of having a new, selfish investment in its future, but because of a shared experience with others who have lived through the bizarre process of parenting another human. Not that everyone's experience is the same, or that we all approach it in the same way, but I suspect that anyone who has cared for a baby full-time has at least glimpsed complete insanity.

"because of the time which separates the moment when they are written—when only I can see them—from the moment when they will be read by other people, a moment which I feel will never come."[41]

"Bullshit," someone said. "I don't believe that for one minute."

This startled me. Why not? I suppose it strains credibility to think that a woman who had at that point written five autobiographical books and already received at least one prize (though not yet the Nobel) would not be well aware that her words would be read. I, however, had found Ernaux's claim deeply relatable—the idea of other people reading things I have written (yes, including this) is always somewhat unreal to me. But now I wondered: Is this a false modesty on my part, or some kind of magical thinking, a protective charm warding off the self-consciousness that could make writing impossible?

The moment when my engagement with *Simple Passion* shifted from wary, slightly annoyed attention to enthralled absorption was when Ernaux mentioned that when waiting for her lover to arrive,

41. Ernaux, 20.

she would write on a sheet of paper the date and time and "he's going to come," and a variety of feelings about it (fears that he wouldn't, or that his feelings had changed).[42] Then later, she would write on the same sheet, "he came," and some details of the encounter (almost none of which are given in the book, funnily enough). This introduced the question of the relationship between the event and its writing ("I would stare at the scrawls on the paper and the two paragraphs written before and after, which one read in succession without a break. In between them there had been words and gestures that made everything else seem trivial, including the very writing designed to capture them"), which generally fascinates me. But it was also a tantalizing glimpse into the life of a real writer, something that I never feel myself to be. Is this what it's like? You just write things down as they are happening to you?

It was this same detail that, to someone in my book club, added a note of inauthenticity by making

---

42. Ernaux, 10.

it clear that this was a person who was always aware of the public eye, like an early prototype of the social media influencer. But this belief seemed ungentlemanly to me, somehow. It was as if the pleasure (value?) of the book depended on taking the author at her word. Or maybe it was more simple, that I wanted to think of the author as selflessly devoted to the holy art of writing rather than clamoring for attention. But does anyone ever truly write for themselves alone?

For a while, I started trying to take notes during my book club meetings. In part, it's because I was writing this book and was frustrated at how difficult it was to remember precisely how the conversation had proceeded, or the exact words someone had said when I was trying to quote them.[43] But I gave up pretty quickly—it took me out of the conversation

43. The scenes I've been describing should therefore be treated as fictions, though I have tried to represent my memory of them faithfully (and funnily enough, one of the things I have learned since becoming a parent is that I am absolutely terrible at making up stories).

too much. And seemed against the spirit of the thing, somehow.

Our idea of knowledge tends to be limited to things we can capture and hand off to others, something very cerebral.[44] Whatever kind of knowledge is produced in these book club conversations, it's not of the variety that must be, or even can be, recorded in the moment, but rather, one that ripens over time, out of the haziness of your recollections and the imprint of a certain look, or laugh, in a given moment.

I wrote those lines some eight months ago, and I believed them. I still do. But the fundamental contradiction is that I *am* trying to write this book, and it *does* require actually writing—not necessarily taking notes at book club meetings, though I do occasionally

---

44. Katherine McKittrick discusses these various kinds of knowledge and describes Black studies as a different way of knowing. "By observing how arranging, rearranging, and collecting ideas outside ourselves are processes that make our ideas our own, I think about how our ideas are bound up in stories, research, inquiries, that we do not (or should not claim we) own." *Dear Science and Other Stories* (Duke University Press, 2021), 15.

jot some down, these days, but eventually putting my thoughts and impressions into words. And for me, at least, the ability to do so expands with practice: the more often I write, the easier it comes, the more I find that I am able to move among ideas, rearrange them, play with them, discover new ones. Writing, I have so often told my students, is a process of thought, not a record of thought. Yet, it also *is* a record of at least one version of a thought, which will inevitably change later and appear alien, strange. It turns out to be incredibly helpful to keep those scraps of initial impressions and opinions, before they shift and evolve.

I suppose that this is what I want to believe Ernaux is after as well—trying to find words for some kind of experience, or understanding, that resists them. Not to show off or be admired, but to get at the thing, to understand it. Do you have to buy into that idea to enjoy her work? I thought so, but hearing someone else's skepticism made me reconsider.

In that college class on autobiography that I took with Roger Porter, I became absolutely fascinated by the problem of how to turn a life into a book. I followed the course with an independent study on autobiography of illness and disability, which gave me the excuse to read even more autobiographies (I read forty of them that semester) and loads of studies on autobiographical writing, and gradually I came to understand that what I was actually interested in was not autobiography at all, but narrative, and fiction. I realized that I was not only uninterested in but also actively annoyed by the question of autobiographical truth. *Who cares if it is true?* I thought. *All I care about is whether it's a compelling book.* Yes, I was disgusted by outright liars, or frauds—this was the era of the James Frey *Million Little Pieces* Oprah debacle, such scandals were at a premium—but I had no desire to spend my time obsessing over factuality. I really came to believe this about myself: that whether or not a book was fiction didn't much matter to me. But when someone in our group said that she hated *Simple Passion* and might have liked it more if she had realized it was a memoir, I instantly understood that I too would have found the book uninteresting, probably unbearable, if it had been a novel. Not so much because of the obsessive protagonist—she might have been challenging, but she isn't that different from some of Elena Ferrante's characters, and I like reading about them just fine—but because what I really care about in the book is what the narrator says about writing it. What makes it interesting is how the narrator is trying to find the words and way to describe it; that's the real story, for me. If that part isn't real, what is left?

In a class, you are supposed to take notes, because you are supposed to be learning something. That might be the most obvious difference between book club and classroom—the expectation that people are recording the things they hear in order to review them later.

But then my friend Barry shares on Facebook that he is experimenting with a new approach to seminars where there is no technology allowed, not even a phone on the table, and no note taking. His friends are intrigued. He reports that his students are very happy with the results; that they feel a real sense of connection; that the conversations are much better because everyone is far more present. Shy students seem more willing to speak, to take risks, because no one is writing anything down. There is no memory work; the point is to engage the book and the concepts, and each other.

But they still write papers afterward. I wonder if the prompts are different, or if he has noticed a difference in the kinds of things they write. I should ask him.

In the literature classroom, the teacher has notes, a lesson plan. Do they? Mine vary. Usually I have my notes about the text—mostly a list of key passages with page numbers, so that I can find them easily during class, and a series of questions. Only rarely do I have a specific activity in mind. Sometimes, yes—on the first day discussing *The Epic of Gilgamesh*, we will always go over the first two pages of the text and make a list of the heroic qualities being celebrated and consider what they tell us about the function of a leader, and on the first day of *Mrs. Dalloway* we will read the first two paragraphs and carefully note the shifts in perspective and time. But mostly, I'm improvising. Looking at my teaching notes now, they are largely incomprehensible to me, useless unless I've just finished rereading the text (which is how I prepare for every class).

Sometimes I don't even have notes—something I recognize now as a sign of pure overwhelm, that I had read for class in a hurry and couldn't even find a moment to jot down a few thoughts. Those are the days when I enter the classroom with a feeling of cold dread, terrified at the possibility that there will be nothing to say. But often, those end up being really excellent classes. A chance remark will spark an idea or a thread of inquiry, and I'll follow it, because I have nothing else to do, so my students will see me genuinely thinking out loud, really weighing their ideas, rather than using them as stepping stones to my own points. Whatever mass of work I'm buried under will generally prevent me from taking notes even afterward, and anyway, it's very hard to reconstruct what was said. But those ideas do stay in my brain, somewhere.

I was teaching Marjane Satrapi's *Chicken with Plums* for the second time recently, having first taught it almost six years ago and left myself only the scantest of notes (mostly documenting the way that the text charts the passage of time—with specific dates in some places and in relative terms like "one month later" or "one week later" in others. But why was I tracking this? "Representations of time," say my notes, cryptically). As I was standing at the front of the room talking, I had a sudden jolt of recognition—stronger than déjà vu; a sense of certainty that I most definitely *had* had this idea before, that the book is a fascinating play on Aristotelian tragedy. Just like in Aristotle's definition, the protagonist of *Chicken with Plums* is "a man who is not eminently good and just, yet whose misfortune is brought about not by vice or depravity, but by some error or frailty."[45] This is because, I explain to my class, the story of bad things happening to bad people isn't tragic, it's justice, and the story of bad

45. Aristotle, *Poetics*.

things happening to good people isn't satisfying, it's shocking, terrifying. So the person must be somehow in between (because bad things must happen, that's what makes it a tragedy). Aristotle says also that the protagonist should be someone "highly renowned and prosperous," or at least an "illustrious" man from a good family, which is sort of amusing when you consider that the story is about Satrapi's great uncle.

Back when I was teaching at Bilkent University, I would spend every fall semester thinking about tragedy, working through *Oedipus Rex*, *Antigone*, the movie *Chinatown*, and Beckett's *Act Without Words I*. What was perpetually fascinating to me was the way all of them pondered the question of fate and inevitability, giving you just enough of a sense of agency to make the disastrous outcomes feel almost avoidable—a twist of the knife. This was on my mind now as I pointed out to my students that Satrapi too was playing with the question of fate and determinism. Yes, Nasser Ali Khan decides to end his life, but look at his conversation with the Angel of Death on the Sixth Day! When it's your time, it's your time!

If we had already been thinking about the nature of tragedy, it would have been fun to consider how *Chicken with Plums* subverts Aristotle's ideas about the proper arrangement of events in a plot; how it scrambles the order of the beginning, middle, and end, and what this does to the sense of cause and effect. Was this why I had mentioned the representation of time in my notes? The question ran through my mind as I was speaking. But now I linked the time markers, instead, to genre and realism. We had been discussing how the book feels like a folktale—the pared-down detail (even the way the figures seemed to float in a blank background, abstracted out of any specific setting); the slightly supernatural quality of a person deciding to die and then dying one week later; the forthright yet laconic meditations on spirituality and meaning. The dogged reminders of specific dates and unexpected leaps into the present were a jarring insistence that this story is *real*, these people existed.[46] This is what gives the book its unique, strange quality—we are primed to read it as some kind of

46. Though ironically, it is at least somewhat fictionalized—names have been changed.

mythic work, detached from the world we know, but these details demand that we at least consider the possibility that it's meant to be a factual account.

So, I mused, we should take seriously the possibility that the Angel of Death is an actual character, not just a symbol. What would it be like to truly believe this? Is this the work of bridging cultural difference? *We* don't believe in things like the Angel of Death, but if *those people, over there* do, we should try to entertain the possibility, ostensibly so that we can engage with their tradition respectfully?

It seems worth noting, I said, that this book was published in 2004, in a post–9/11 world that was absolutely roiling with Islamophobia.[47] Not that mainstream American views of Iran are all that rosy even today, but at the time it was more clearly in the spotlight as part of the 'Axis of Evil,' deeply foreign and frightening. It's hard not to suspect that Satrapi

47. Here I realized, with a twinge, that the people I was speaking to were born after 2001 and had no memory of a pre-9/11 world. I want to believe that they have been exposed to the fact that plenty of Americans are Muslims and that hijab is a normal part of some people's attire, such that they find it hard to comprehend the extent to which the veil was one of the foremost symbols of women's oppression in the mid-2000s, but maybe this is overly optimistic of me.

was consciously making the book into something of an ambassador, and including anecdotes like the story of the five men inspecting the elephant because they might be familiar to readers and help them form other kinds of mental maps (my students nodded thoughtfully).

It may seem condescending, I went on, but this is how people typically conceptualize the ways that literature teaches us empathy and the value of diversity. Perhaps we could put it another way, then: What if this book is trying to help us shed our ignorance and see the world as it really is? As in, it is telling us about the Angel of Death so that we can prepare for our own eventual encounter with him? Because if you really think that the benefit of the book is that it shows you how other people perceive the world, then shouldn't that benefit include you taking those beliefs seriously, rather than dismissing them as colorful detail? My students froze.

Or maybe it really is just a fiction, I continued, and we should be careful about taking any single text as representative of the beliefs or worldview of large groups of people? People shifted uncomfortably in their seats, looked troubled.

The point is, I said, flailing for some kind of conclusion to this runaway tangent I had heedlessly embarked upon, to notice these different aspects of genre, and how they link up with larger patterns of thought or systems of belief. Part of what makes this book so fascinating is that it brings together these different modes that we experience as slightly discordant, consistently surprising us and unsettling our approach to reading it. What I want you to notice is how this happens; how the book works.

I wasn't really planning to end up there, but in another way, this is where I always end up, the only thing I ever really teach. *Notice what the book is doing. How does it do that?*

My friend Nathan posts to social media about teaching Richard McGuire's incredible graphic novel, *Here*, and mentions that he's taught it almost every semester since I told him about it on a road trip we took together to a conference in 2018. I think, *Maybe this is one of the most significant ways that I have impacted the world?* Not by teaching *Here* myself—though I have, several times—but by getting it into the hands of someone who can *really* teach?

I'm joking, sort of, but it's also true that I am far more comfortable with the idea that I have persuaded someone to read a book, who will then persuade many other people to do so, than I am with the idea that there are a hundred or so people out there who have learned the book from me, as it were—that their take on it is molded from my own impressions.

Yet, as my friend Alexis points out, reading a draft of *this* book, what am I doing with all these vignettes about various texts? Am I not teaching them to you?

My friend Teagan and I are having drinks at a picnic table on the back patio of a bar, on what feels like it is probably the last really pleasantly warm day of the year, before we are beset by the cold and the dark that can seem endless in Ithaca, and we are talking about our work, and how we both are frequently doing extremely close readings of books that we assume our audience probably has not read. "Can I ask you something?" she says, and I lean forward, curious. "Has anyone ever told you that they read a book that you wrote about because your interpretation made them want to?"

I search my memory. "I don't think so? People regularly say that they plan to, usually tied to some guilt about not having read Polish authors. But I don't know if anyone ever actually has. What about you?"

"Yeah," she says, "once. And they told me afterward that it was really disappointing, because what I had said was so much more interesting than the book itself."

We both laugh, because we know that this is probably true.

I'm frankly somewhat appalled by the idea that anyone would seek out some of the books I write about and try to read them for pleasure. They're not exactly … fun. I mean, they are to me, in a perverse sort of way, because I'm caught by their strangeness; they're a puzzle that I can't put down, but I don't really think that other people would relish them, most of the time anyway. For one thing, I don't think people read eighteenth- and nineteenth-century novels for fun all that often, and that's mostly what I write about. But even when fellow academics say that they intend to read one of the books I've discussed, I get slightly uncomfortable, and will often laughingly tell them that it's not necessary.

So why would they want to read what I have to say about those books? Because my arguments tend to be, more broadly, claims about how fiction makes meaning—whatever text I'm discussing is but one example; there could be others. You don't have to read this one, unless perhaps you want to check my work. But actually, it doesn't really matter if you disagree with me about that particular book; if you do, you can write your own essay offering a different interpretation, and I will gladly read it. This, perhaps, is what it means to be a scholar of literature: that you can be not only interested but even invested in arguments about books that you haven't even read. And that you disagreeing with my interpretation does not mean that I am incorrect.[48]

Because in stark contrast to my teaching, in my academic writing I really am trying to persuade someone, and I am stubbornly adamant in wanting them to agree with me. I am convinced of my own rightness and ready to fight about it.

Some years after I got my PhD, I came to learn that the institution that granted it to me was infamous for its culture of vicious interrogations after lectures. This revelation filled me with social anxiety: Was I asking cruel, humiliating questions at conferences and lectures without even realizing it? What kinds of questions should one ask after a talk?

48. In this vein, Jonathan Kramnick discusses the idea that replicability is not a measure of accuracy in literary criticism in *Criticism and Truth*.

But it also taught me to recognize what I was only dimly aware of in graduate school: the way that my whole body thrills to a good lecture and a slightly heated debate about ideas.

There is the sadistic version of this: the pleasure of tearing into a weak argument as a kind of blood sport, and the sense of smug pleasure when you have won. And of course, it is also a form of peacocking and jostling for status. The university that trained me has its uglier side. But I cannot entirely let go of the notion that at the heart of it is a passionate and unabashed commitment to ideas that exists there in a rare and beautiful form.[49]

Maybe the thing I most love about book clubs is that they assign reading to me. I like homework. And I especially like being made to read a book that I otherwise wouldn't.

49. As this book heads to press, this belief has been dealt a devastating blow by the announcement that they are pausing graduate admissions to a whole raft of programs in the humanities, particularly those that involve teaching other languages, and including the department that educated me.

A logistical tangent: How does one pick books for a book club? Ideally you have a group of people with somewhat different tastes, because the discussion is better when they don't all agree. This means that they won't necessarily want to read the same kinds of things. Personally, I like a system where everyone gets a turn, not to pick, but to nominate three books that the others vote on. It seems like a good balance of choice and coercion. But having so much logistical armature can be off-putting, so sometimes it's better to keep things more informal—people just propose stuff, and eventually you coalesce around a selection.

I often think of myself as someone who reads widely and eclectically, but I increasingly recognize that this is an illusion. There are many, many books that I have very little interest in. And I feel slightly guilty about this disinterest, and take it as a kind of penance to read one of these books and make a real effort to appreciate it.

It's also pleasantly disorienting to me to start on a

book that I know absolutely nothing about.[50] The Big-City Women chose Alma Guillermoprieto's *Dancing with Cuba*, and I launched in without even reading the jacket flap. It starts out as a memoir about being a young Mexican woman struggling to make it as a ballet dancer in New York City (the descriptions of dance are wonderful), and then there's a swerve: she accepts a position to teach at a ballet school in Cuba.

Here the book becomes somewhat confused. Is it trying to capture what life was like in Cuba in 1970? Does it want the reader to understand how a person could really feel drawn to the Communist cause, and even be electrified during a many-hours-long speech by Castro? Or is the point rather to depict how a twenty-one-year-old could be largely oblivious to the political realities around her because she was so consumed by the emotional melodrama of a long-distance

50. Another way to give yourself this experience is to become a subscriber to an independent press, so that books will just appear in your mailbox, like Kafka's Imperial Message. I subscribe to New York Review of Books, & Other Stories, Open Letter, New Directions, Archipelago, and Deep Vellum. This is of course completely untenable as far as reading them right away, but also means that even if I did know something about one of the books, there's such an onslaught that I'll probably forget by the time I pick it up.

relationship with a man who, in retrospect, seemed highly mediocre? These are different angles the book could take, and unfortunately, they are somewhat at odds with each other, and the author never chooses between them.

But I don't regret reading the book. It was an interesting failure. And the conversation about it, particularly a debate that emerged over whether or not Guillermoprieto was more self-absorbed or shallow than any other twenty-one-year-old might be, helped me understand why: we couldn't figure out how the book wanted us to feel about the protagonist because the author herself didn't seem to know how she felt about her past and the decisions she had made. This meant that she didn't know what story she wanted to tell. The book's "hook," young woman goes to Cuba to teach in a ballet school, was promising, but it never quite coalesced into an idea.

Still, I learned some things by reading it, and various scenes have lodged in my mind. One never knows when they will resurface, or how they will attach to another thought, shape a new reflection. I've been working on an essay, an unexpected side project, pondering a scene in his memoir where Olaudah Equiano—a man who was kidnapped and sold into slavery during the eighteenth century and eventually became emancipated and then, after many travels, settled in London—mentions that he wants to go to Turkey. Why Turkey? I wondered. And how to interpret his seemingly casual statement, after visiting it, that "In general I believe they are fond of black people"[51]—a claim that seems questionable in the eighteenth century, and honestly, even still today? As I started pondering these questions, I found myself drawing together ideas from a variety of different texts that I've read, many of them semirandomly, at very different points in my life: Kader Konuk's *East West Mimesis: Auerbach in Turkey*; Magdalena Zaborowska's *James Baldwin's Turkish Decade: Erotics of Exile*; Katherine McKittrick's *Dear Science and Other Stories*; an essay by Namwali Serpell called "Unbothered." I'm still figuring out the connections among them—I guess

---

51. Olaudah Equiano, *The Interesting Narrative of the Life of Olaudah Equiano*, ed. Angelo Costanzo (Broadview Press, 2001), 184.

that's part of what the essay is about, now, is how they fit together, aside from the fact that I happen to have read them all—but what it has given me to understand is that reading books is like planting seeds in this brain of mine. Unexpected things will grow from the strange and eclectic collection of texts.

Jonathan Kramnick argues that close reading is really a kind of writing. This may seem surprising (it was to me): so many arguments about literary studies describe it as a kind of reading, characterized by an "ideal of attentiveness," a specific kind of noticing.[52] I do it myself—I've done it here, in reverse, when I was worrying about whether I can read the way other people do. I was assuming that there is something specific about the way I read that is scholarly, trained, and that cannot be undone.

But Kramnick suggests that we should see close reading, instead, as a form of writing. The point is

52. Jonathan Kramnick, *Criticism and Truth: On Method in Literary Studies* (University of Chicago Press, 2023), 35.

not only that it is a particular genre with its own conventions and norms, but also that it requires a certain skill, developed precisely in order to produce this craftwork, this written thing.

What this illuminates for me is that I don't read in some particular way that scholars do. I notice features that the average person might not, yes, and I can connect them to a larger history of texts and forms of writing. But the way I do so is unique to me. We don't all see the same things or understand them the same way. The arguments that I make about books are very different from those of my colleagues, even if I write in the way we have all been trained to do, not only because they arise from the particular clusters of things that I have read, the seeds I have planted, but also because the things I notice and care about are often different from those that excite them, and even when they are similar, I may connect them differently, landing somewhere else.

The reading, the conversations, and the writing. All different.

I attended a conference recently where I went to a panel organized around a newly published novel, one rather outside of my normal fields of study. In the days leading up to it, I read the book, which was complicated and interesting. I got even more excited about the panel, eager to be taught something, to see how a handful of smart people with expertise in various related areas would read this novel.

But the panel was a disappointment. I felt like I couldn't really understand most of the papers—whether this is because I lack the necessary expertise in those subfields; because I struggle to track arguments delivered out loud, especially complex ones; or because many of them didn't really have a clear point or argument, is an open question. The one paper that I did understand, and liked, situated the novel in relation to the author's previous work and talked about how his earlier books, which were clearly set in and engaging with specific political and historical contexts, might have staked out controversial and even unappealing positions on those contexts, but at least they had actual stakes. The later work, she argued, was drained of meaningful reference, seemingly for the sake of abstract contemplation, but the results seemed toothless, and much less satisfying than the politically disappointing stuff that preceded it. A very interesting and persuasive account, but one that did not give me much to chew on in relation to *this* novel.

I felt sort of let down and frustrated. I want to dig into this novel more, to turn it upside down and give it a good shaking and see what falls out of its pockets. I looked up some reviews (although I didn't want to *read* more, I wanted to talk to people, wanted conversation!) and they were bland, descriptive. A week later, I met with my book club of big-city women to discuss something else, and tried to persuade them to read the novel. No dice. They'd read three other books by that author and had no interest in another. I called my mom and told her to read it, but she has an entire shelf teeming with books that I have demanded that she read so as to talk to me about them, so who knows when she'll get to this one.

So what is left for me? I'll write a blog post about it.[53] I'll talk to myself. But not in the way I talk to other academics, in my official research. This, I understand now, is what my various book clubs have taught me: a new way that I've learned to write, not an "official" writing, but a kind of thinking-on-paper, a dialogue with myself that is built in part out of a discussion I'm having in my mind with all kinds of other people. It's on the page rather than out loud, so I can take a little longer to say things, and throw in some quotes (admittedly I do that out loud too sometimes, but it can get cumbersome). It's not my academic writing, but it's not based in some mystical, other form of reading that is separate from the one that feeds my scholarship, it's just that it's part of a different conversation, so the way that I'm speaking is different too.

It's the way I talk to you.

—Ithaca, January 2024

53. www.kasiareads.com/blog/.

Acknowledgments

Thanks must go first to Jeff Deutsch, who asked me to write this and told me to take all the time I wanted doing it—an incredible act of faith and generosity, and really, the only way this book could have come to be. And then, of course, to all the people who have read with me over the years, in classrooms and outside them, and shared their thoughts, and helped me form mine. It would take pages and pages to name them all, but you know who you are, and I dedicate this to you.

I also need to thank Matthew Engelke and Connor Martini for shepherding my work through the process of publication, and for being wonderfully encouraging at every step of the way. And my skillful copyeditor, Leslie Kriesel, who did valiant battle (sometimes unsuccessfully, I'm sorry to say) with my absurdly excessive comma usage and love of dashes.

I want to keep this short, so I can't mention every person who helped bring this book to life, but I do have to name a few beloved individuals who read various pieces and offered helpful suggestions (some of which

I didn't take, but certainly should have), or listened to random stories and said, "You have to write about this"—especially Alexis Becker, Dyani Johns Taff, Jen Spitzer, Chris Holmes, Bethany Dixon, Teagan Bradway, Elisha Cohn, and Kevin Quashie. Big thanks also to Mary Mullen and the wonderful students in her class on reading communities, who made me feel like a celebrity rather than homework. And my Squad, Stephanie Insley Hershinow, Kathy Lubey, and Eugenia Zuroski, who make me smarter and braver and better.

But for this book especially, I really have to thank all the people in my life who aren't academics, and who keep insisting that they really are interested in the stuff I think and write about, with such loving enthusiasm that I even start to believe them. Keyana and Martin Medina, and Rosie and Dan Finelli—you didn't have to be my family, but how lucky for me that you are. And Jake Spicer, who told me once with genuine sorrow in his voice that it would really be too bad if all of my writing ended up being academic—I think it changed my life.

And of course, gratitude always to Aleksandra Jasińska-Kania, whose own memoirs helped me understand that my life might be interesting, and Joanna Kania-Bartoszyńska and Tomek Bartoszyński, who made me the reader I am and who, incredibly, keep reading the various texts I pass on to them. And to Antonio Perry, who has all of my heart, and is generous enough to share it (and every room of our house) with all the books. And finally, Julian Bartoszyński Perry, my favorite person to read with.

About the Author

Katarzyna Bartoszyńska is a writer, translator, and academic. A graduate of Reed College and the University of Chicago, she is currently an Associate Professor of Literatures in English and Women's, Gender, and Sexuality Studies at Ithaca College. More of her work can be found at www.kasiareads.com.